WITHDRAWN

Schaumburg Township District Library

130 South Roselle Road

Schaumburg, Illinois 60193

The
Arrival
of the
Future

B. H. FAIRCHILD

Alice James Books
Farmington, Maine

SCHAUMBURG TOWNSHIP DISTRICT LIBRARY
130 SOUTH ROSELLE ROAD
SCHAUMBURG, ILLINOIS 60193

B 11
FAIRCHILD, B

LIBRARY OF CONGRESS CATALOGING-IN-PUBLICATION-DATA

Fairchild, B. H.
The arrival of the future / B. H. Fairchild
p. cm.
ISBN 1-882295-25-0 (pbk.)
I. Title

PS 3556.A3625 A88 2000
811'.54--dc21   00-024412

Alice James Books gratefully acknowledges support from
the University of Maine at Farmington
and the National Endowment for the Arts.

Alice James Books are published by the Alice James Poetry Cooperative, Inc.,
an affiliate of the University of Maine at Farmington.
Alice James Books
98 Main Street
Farmington, Maine 04938

www.umf.maine.edu/~ajb

for my mother and father

Contents

3 1257 01471 5667

Preface

I am deeply indebted to Alice James Books for the republication of *The Arrival of the Future*, my first full-length book of poems, which was originally published in 1985 by Swallow's Tale Press as a result of winning their annual poetry competition, established and conducted at great expense, effort, and self-sacrifice by the publisher and writer, Joe Taylor. Unfortunately, soon after the appearance of the book, the Press ceased doing business, and *The Arrival of the Future* has been difficult to find or out of print for some time. It is wonderful to have it revived by Alice James Books with the cover painting, *The Wasp Killers*, by my old and close friend, Don Radke.

Some of the poems contained herein were written as long as thirty years ago, and so the process of retyping them has brought back memories of those same years when my wife, Patricia, and I were living in very modest accommodations in Kearney, Nebraska; Tulsa, Oklahoma; and San Marcos, Texas. Just as memory is, to some degree, a revisionary process, so it has been tempting to revise a few of these poems—certain lines or phrases here and there—but that would be untrue to the original book, which should stand again as it once was. I have, however, corrected numerous typographical errors, slightly altered one title for clarity, and included some notes and this preface. So here again, rescued from the past in order to arrive in the future, is *The Arrival of the Future*.

Part One

What can we do with the plains' beaten weight?
No one can believe the slow hunger in them.
We think it's theirs, the vast flatness, but on the journey
To sleep, there it is in ourselves, there it is.

OSIP MANDELSTAM (trans. W. S. Merwin)

Machine Shop with Wheat Field

East behind the shop, junk:
hunks of iron turning to rust, mud pumps,
rat-hole diggers, drill collars, odd lengths of pipe lying
in bunch grass blown by a nervous wind.
A boy sleeps on a traveling block.

Lathes from the shop make small
shrieks as bits hit metal, digging out a
level groove, then lowering to a rumble. Long
coils of blue steel smoke, hissing as they
slither into oil and water.

The machinist in blue
who chain-smokes Lucky Strikes leans against his
tool box and watches through a grease-smeared window
rows of wheat lean with each gust of wind.
He thinks of threshers drawn by horses.

All four machinists set
their lathes and settle back with cigarettes.
They listen to the clang and scrape of hoist chains
along the pipe racks. The huge shop doors
creak, and sparrows chatter overhead.

The boy dreams in photographs
of men posed along a horse-drawn thresher,
hats held thigh-level, all in overalls. A boy,
his father, rides one of the horses.
Behind them, wheat bends in rows.

The afternoon sun forms
a square of light on the shop floor. The square
lengthens until the shop becomes a world of light,
and the men begin to leave, casting
long shadows, lathes sighing to a halt.

The waking boy forgets
his dream and stares across the wheat field at
the lowering sun. The blue machinist waves at him,
his hand's shadow touching field and boy,
who walks toward the blazing shop.

The Men

As a kid sitting in a yellow vinyl
booth in the back of Earl's Tavern,
you watch the late-afternoon drunks
coming and going, sunlight breaking
through the smoky dark as the door
opens and closes, and it's the future
flashing ahead like the taillights
of a semi as you drop over a rise
in the road on your way to Amarillo,
bright lights and blonde-haired women,
as Billy used to say, slumped over
his beer like a snail, *make a real man*
out of you, the smile bleak as the gaps
between his teeth, *stay loose, son,*
don't die before you're dead. Always
the warnings from men you worked with
before they broke, blue fingernails,
eyes red as fate. *A different life*
for me, you think, and outside later,
feeling young and strong enough to raise
the sun back up, you stare down Highway 54,
pushing everything—stars, sky, moon,
all but a thin line at the edge
of the world—behind you. Your headlights
sweep across the tavern window,
ripping the dark from the small, humped
shapes of men inside who turn and look,
like small animals caught in the glare
of your lights on the road to Amarillo.

Angels

Elliot Ray Neiderland, home from college
one winter, hauling a load of Herefords
from Hogtown to Guymon with a pint of
Ezra Brooks and a copy of Rilke's *Duineser
Elegien* on the seat beside him, saw the ass-end
of his semi gliding around in the side mirror
as he hit ice and knew he would never live
to see graduation or the castle at Duino.

In the hospital, head wrapped like a gift
(the nurses had stuck a bow on top), he said
four flaming angels crouched on the hood, wings
spread so wide he couldn't see, and then
the world collapsed. We smiled and passed a flask
around. Little Bill and I sang *Your Cheatin'
Heart* and laughed, and then a sudden quiet
put a hard edge on the morning and we left.

Siehe, ich lebe, Look, I'm alive, he said,
leaping down the hospital steps. The nurses
waved, white dresses puffed out like pigeons
in the morning breeze. We roared off in my Dodge,
Behold, I come like a thief! he shouted to the town
and gave his life to poetry. He lives, now,
in the south of France. His poems arrive
by mail, and we read them and do not understand.

Black Bear Creek

When Black Bear rose on the Oto,
the sky popped like an old tire
and lightning ripped at the seams.
The earth's growl and a mad cracking of trees
brought your father from the tin milk shed.

I see you there, child,
dirty white dress ballooning in the wind,
blue mouth wide behind blown-down hair.
Chickens squawked, horses skittered in the barn,
and the far moan of Holsteins
made you clap your ears.

Afterwards, watching water dark as blood
stirred by splintered limbs,
you knew what time could bring:
the quickness of calamity,
disaster's rise and fall,

and things unseen, the son who dreamed
again and again of black water
reaching over red Oklahoma dirt
and the spreading wetness in his shoes
that could not move, could not save him
from some creeping darkness, something like a flood.

Night Shift

On the down side
of the night shift:
the wind's tense sigh,
the heavy swivel
turning, turning.
Pulling out of the hole
from four thousand feet
straight down,
we change bits, the moon
catching in the old one
a yellow gleam wedged
in mud, a shark's tooth.
The drawworks rumbles
like a flood rushing over
flat stubble fields
that stretch for miles,
all surface, no depth
until now, swept under
ocean, the moon wavering
behind clouds
like a floating body
seen from underwater.
I see small eyes,
feel the hard gray skin
slipping past, and think
of origins, the distances
of time, the absence
of this rig, these men.
On the long drive home

I'll head into a sun
that stared the sea away,
that saw a dried tooth
sink into the darkness
I return to.

Kansas Avenue

a sequence of five poems

I. THE ROBINSON HOTEL

The windows form a sun in white squares.
   Across the street
the Bluebird Café leans into shadow and the cook
   stands in the doorway.
Men from harvest crews step from the Robinson
   in clean white shirts
and new jeans. They stroll beneath the awning,
   smoking Camels,
considering the blue tattoos beneath their sleeves,
   Friday nights
in San Diego years ago, a woman, pink neon lights
   rippling in rain water.
Tonight, chicken-fried steak and coffee alone
   at the Bluebird,
a double feature at The PLAZA: *The Country Girl,*
   The Bridges at Toko-Ri.
The town's night-soul, a marquee flashing orange
   bulbs, stuns the windows
of the Robinson. The men will leave as heroes,
   undiscovered.
Their deaths will be significant and beautiful
   as bright aircraft,
sun glancing on silver wings, twisting, settling
   into green seas.
In their rooms at night, they see Grace Kelly
   bending at their bedsides.
They move their hands slowly over their chests
   and raise their knees
against the sheets. The PLAZA'S orange light

fills the curtains.
Cardboard suitcases lie open, white shirts folded
like pressed flowers.

II. HUMPY'S NEWSSTAND

Your den of paperbacks on Kansas Avenue
swarmed with darknesses and boys dizzy
for knowledge. Gross, mysterious, you slumped
behind the counter, smoking gargantuan cigars
and plotting horse trades and land deals.
Your wealth was legend, your power sinister:
every lurking husband needing rubbers waited
for your grunting hulk to hand them over.

From the Robinson Hotel harvest crews
would pour, the ones with frightened eyes
sliding from the light to where thick-
buttocked girls shone from racks of magazines
in back. You watched us, not them. We fell
to books marked "CLASSICS": *Brave New World,*
The Martian Chronicles, and the poet Sebastian,
who saw the face of God and was devoured.

Your one obsession was a brother, James, who
shot himself: how a man can lose his life
before it's lost. We sat still on unwrapped
stacks of *Time* and *Life* while you vanished
in a cloud. At dusk we lined the curb.
Husbands slinked down dusty streets, rubbers
round as planets stuffed deep in thigh pockets,
new worlds glowing secret possibilities.

III. THE BLUEBIRD CAFÉ

Morning light would strike our coffee cups
and our curled palms would seem to hold
a small blaze. And so our working days
would burn to a dead end—a night of pool,
too many beers, sleep—and begin again at
the Bluebird Café. The no-name cook
fried eggs, bacon, and gallons of grease
to the twang and whine of Flatt and Scruggs.

Earl Talbot, the iron man of Hogtown, hung
out there. And old Mulie. And LuAnne,
Mulie's wife, who waited tables in a snood
and tennis shoes. Some nights I brought
a pint of Ezra Brooks. We drank and sang
and LuAnne danced sometimes until she cried.
The next day Earl and Mulie sat quietly while
LuAnne served four boys whose hands held fire.

IV. Shorty's Pool Hall

In my dream the old men are dogs,
lumps of brown snores spilling
over the back-room floor.
The young men stalk green fields
with cues like knives and die
bravely in the stench-filled restroom
everyone refused. When I wake,
I rub blue dust from my fingertips.

The old men and their stories:
how the Law came to No Man's Land.
Ed Russell, who read *Decline of
the West* nine times, said it came
the way it always did: rustlers got
rich, then brought the Law to save
themselves from rustlers. Ed sighed
and the old men boozed in shadows.

In late afternoon we would pause
as sunlight slanting through the big
front window filled amber bottles
lined along the sill, and the pool hall
swelled into a huge cathedral silence.
The old men would rise from darkened
tables, hands gathering dominoes
like wheat, the day's late harvest.

V. The PLAZA

> I think of cinemas, panoramic sleights
> With multitudes bent toward some flashing scene
> Never disclosed, but hastened to again.
>   HART CRANE, "To Brooklyn Bridge"

The wrecked marquee, edged with rows
of empty sockets, broken bulbs.
My last time here the letters spelled out
Moby Dick, or was it *Creature
from the Black Lagoon?*   Posters, stills
long gone, box office boarded up
where fat Wanda brooded, slumped
on her stool behind loops of pastel
tickets, me inside in crimson blazer
and black plastic bow tie, dispensing
stubs and 3-D glasses—one lens red,
the other blue—to what the manager
liked to call the clientele. Now
I climb the rusting fire escape
that zigzags to the balcony,
whose exit door breathes slowly open
like every door that Hitchcock left
unlocked. The wool air clings. I stop
to test the sagging floor. Far back
rats skitter in the ancient dark
where once a trembling beam of light
hovered above soul-kissing lovers
in the back row. My ex-usher's eyes
clear the gloom, and climbing stairs
I come into the heart of dark
and light. The projectionist read
fuck books here, rising now and then

to change the reel or turn the sound
back up. In *Key Largo* once
he let the motor die, lamp on,
the frame's center scorched and spreading
just as Johnny Rocco pleads, "More!
I want more!" Projector gone, fat stack
of Nightstand paperbacks removed,
I kick the shelves for bats and, reaching
under, find old posters smothering
under dust: *The Man from Planet X,
King Solomon's Mines,* the original
Invasion of the Body Snatchers.
Through chinks in windows painted black
I look out on the street below
where lines would form each summer evening,
where strolling up and down, bow tie
gleaming in the sun, I would announce
that all the tickets had been sold,
this feature was the last, and could they
come again tomorrow when *The Day
the Earth Stood Still* began a two-week run.

Moments later standing at the rail,
I lean over a sea of abandoned
seats dim as midnight breakers.
Looking straight across, I stare
into the massive whiteness rising up,
great dumb whale of our dark journeys,
blank face of life's true meaning
beginning, ending, in white silence.
As in the old days I leave slowly,
hearing my steps go down into
the empty house and come back up,
bracing my eyes against the opening door.

Jughead at the SHANGRI-LA

Standing half-lit in jukebox light
and lifted up by whanging songs
and a woman under each arm, you
shouted me out of a dark corner.
Bright cousin, family legend,
inventor of tailless kites and portable
aquariums, steel-skulled running back
and friend to movie stars, why were you there?

Roughnecking your way from rig to rig,
you came from dreamy California
to the only joint in the only town
dead enough to make drunkenness
a virtue. The Rembrandt shadows
of that bar, your portrait by Vermeer
(A Man and Two Women) stuck in my brain,
and now you're gone, that blue scene stays.

Heart halted at forty, you died
in an easy chair in bourgeois
comfort. I remember you
waking up my folks, dazzling us
with tales of cycling over Europe
the Netherlands, pale Luxembourg,
pastel shapes on maps, strange lands
unthinkable as death or Shangri-la.

In the Homes of the Working Class

Everything is here. Linoleum
in alternating squares of red
and gray. Bare wall on the west
rising under an afternoon sun.
Couch in brown vinyl,
empty bottle of Miller High Life,
crucifix over the dinner table.
An odor of sleep and sauerkraut,
fresh laundry and ammonia.

No one is here. The rooms sigh stillness.
Each object has its own end
and possesses itself. Slowly the home
gathers itself under shadows.
Later, the occupants will return,
assuming the burden of possession,
feeling the heaviness of the day's
last light. The objects will relinquish
themselves, trusting in the future.

Portrait of My Father as a Young Man

AFTER RILKE

The unbroken horse, all head, eyes like tunnels,
and you stand there laughing in chaps and bandana,
dangling a lariat with that light grace
only your hands held. Years later at a lathe
among motes and shafts of light, those hands
flickered like fish, chrome handles spinning,
bit gleaming, biting in just deep enough
to hiss and make smoke wisps rise while
your heavy body settled back in its deep
dream of success. You must have thought
of this: the skinny boy, all bones, standing
by the still unbroken stallion. Break life,
this picture said, marry, make sons and money.

The son who grew to see the lathes shut down
now holds the photograph in clumsy hands, searching
for the boy who broke horses for a dollar,
clowned in ten-gallon hats, laughed at failure.

C & W Machine Works

Maybe the light angling over the lathe
made me remember: the dust drifting
in shafts of evening sun, the grease-
and-water smell, the good shine of steel

honed by human hands. The thud-
and-slide of a milling machine pulled
me in. I knew where I was. The time-
clock coughed and I nearly punched in.

This hollow shop. A wide door O'Keeffe
would love and I almost walked by. But now
I breathe stale air, listen to the wind beat
on corrugated tin, and touch cold steel again.

Part Two

. . . on the puzzle
of the nature of desire/ the consequences
in the known world beyond
the terra incognita/ on how men do use
their lives . . .

CHARLES OLSON

Hair

At the 23rd Street Barber Shop
hair is falling across the arms of men,
across white cotton cloths
that drape their bodies like little nightgowns.
How like well-behaved children they seem—
silent, sleepy—sheets tucked
neatly beneath their chins,
legs too short to touch the floor.
Each in his secret life sinks
easily into the fat plastic cushion
and feels the strange lightness of falling hair,
the child's comfort of soft hands
caressing his brow and temples.
Each sighs inwardly to the constant
whisper of scissors about his head,
the razor humming small hymns along his neck.

They've been here a hundred times,
gazed upon mirrors within mirrors,
clusters of slim-necked bottles labeled WILDROOT
and VITALIS, and below the shoeshine stand,
rows of flat gold cans. They've heard
the sudden intimacies, the warmth
of men seduced by grooming: the veteran
confessing an abandoned child in Rome,
men discussing palm-sized pistols,
small enough to snuggle against your stomach.
As children they were told, after you're dead
it keeps on growing, and they've seen themselves
lying in hair long as a young girl's.

Two of them rise and walk slowly out.
Their round heads blaze in the doorway.
They creep into what is left of day, fingertips
touching the short, stiff hairs across their necks.

The Woman at the Laundromat Crying "Mercy"

And the glass eyes of dryers whirl
on either side, the roar just loud enough
to still the talk of women. Nothing
is said easily here. Below the screams
of two kids skateboarding in the aisles
thuds and rumbles smother everything,
even the woman crying *mercy, mercy*.

Torn slips of paper on a board swear
Jesus is the Lord, nude photo sessions
can help girls who want to learn, the price
for Sunshine Day School is affordable,
astrology can change your life, any
life. Long white rows of washers lead
straight as highways to a change machine

that turns dollars into dimes to keep
the dryers running. When they stop,
the women lift the dry things out and hold
the sheets between them, pressing corners
warm as babies to their breasts. In back,
the change machine has jammed and a woman
beats it with her fists, crying *mercy, mercy*.

A Cafeteria in Pasadena

The small nouns
Crying faith . . .
GEORGE OPPEN

Under thickening voices and a clatter
of glass, I scribble words on the tablecloth
while the crowd from St. Barnabas files in.
The old man beside me mumbles his prayer.
A young girl with her parents sits before me
in profile. She wears a plum-colored dress,
white barrettes, and black sandals
and sits rigid as an old woman,
hugging the heavy shawl of silence.

With my last few dollars
I have bought the *Kindertotenlieder,*
and I imagine how the thin, aspiring line
of notes reaches for the beauty of this girl.
Suddenly she turns to me, the far side
of her face a red, scarred mass, the eye
gnarled and sunken. The air stills,
voices break and fall apart.

In that stare is the word within the word,
the white cup, empty, on the white tablecloth,
an old man's speech, rising,
the spiraling song.

Groceries

A woman waits in line and reads
from a book of poems to kill time.

When her items come up to be counted,
the check-out girl greets the book
like a lost child: *The House on Marshland!*

she says, and they share certain lines:
"the late apples, red and gold,/ like words
of another language."

The black belt rolls on. Groceries flow,
coagulate, then begin to spill over: canned
corn, chicken pot pies, oatmeal, garden
gloves, apricots, sliced ham, frozen pizza,
loaves and loaves of bread, and then the eggs,

"the sun is shining, everywhere you turn is luck,"
they sing. Here comes the manager, breathless,
eyes like tangerines, hair in flames.

The Girl in the Booth

Glossy black-and-whites
are out now. Color's in:
blue sky, green grass,
red brick house, and
there they stand, hand
on shoulder, smiling straight
ahead. Sure, I steal
a quick look now and then.
Who can blame me?
In this stupid blue
box with windows
boredom sets in early,
soon enough you're rifling
files of yellow envelopes
stuffed with the little
moments of their lives:
new car, string of trout,
holidays in Hawaii—
bending palm and floral
background—then weddings
and funerals, same bright
bleached faces and some kid
frowning into the ground.
Sometimes, though, the odd
shot: double exposure
of cloud and face, mannequin
with painted crotch,
old guy in the attic
window. So many lie
unclaimed. I wonder,
thumbing through these last
remains, whether death,

divorce, or some unspeakable
disaster left them in
my hands. I try to read
the faces like my Aunt Grace
reads coffee grounds. My life
in their faces. My life
outside this one-room room:
another box of borrowed
images and laughter in cans.
Waiting for some future
to bring back here. To develop.
Something I can hold,
to say: these are mine,
we were there, here it is.

Three Poems after Photographs by Robert Frank

I. 8TH STREET

The golden neon arrow above
the old 8th Street Coffee Lounge
in broken waves of light
flies forward over and over
again. Papers float up
like strange fish, like street
shouts that billow and drift away
as night moves in. Weinstein
drops his newsstand awning
with its mural of Lucky Strikes
and enters the small room
of his other life. Street folks
take their places, backs against
the wall, brown bottles lying
in their laps like babies. Aurelio
begins his evening walk around
the block, mumbling garbled rages
and hitting the bricks with his fists.
Now the whores cluster in bright
sashes and black hose, and cars
pull up, one by one, beneath
the arrow. Each wave of light
stops me like a photograph, then
lets me go, this light on 8th Street
in its dream-flight, never moving.

II. 8th Street Bar

The old couple in the booth
under the mirror, their lives
of work filling the glasses
between them. She speaks,
he in his suit and red shirt
gazing up as if memory
with its gull wings hovered there.
I see them young, nude in bed
after making love, morning
sun turning the curtains
to a white glow like the jukebox
blazing now in the center
of the small dance floor.
In the latticework of shadows
customers lift their drinks
delicately, admiring the gleam
along the rim, the uneven sheen
of the bar's veneer, the long, cool
remove from history. I can grow
old here. Someone will serve me,
will set the green bottle beside
the slender glass, and light will flow
endlessly from jukebox to mirror
to glass to floor. I can enter
the bed of the old couple,
lie between them as their child,
hands across my chest, and watch
the air bend and sag with sunlight.

III. SINGER BEACH

Three women are sleeping on the beach
in the shape of three "5's" perfectly
parallel, knees bent at the same angle,
right arms along their thighs, heads
pillowed by handbags. At their feet
a wire basket spills beer bottles
with gold labels that litter the strand,
flashing like moonlight breakers, then
fading in the morning haze. We danced
all night beneath paper-covered lights
and drank champagne, and they listened
to my poems until the air was drunk
and heavy. Now I've lost my shoes,
and the songs we sang are distant hymns
in my poor memory. In their lavender
hats and black hose they are dreaming,
and their future lives are being born
in places I will never know. It's all
touch and go, waves lapping my feet,
the haze that slowly lifts, shop fronts
on the boardwalk opening in enormous
yawns. Daylight starts its slow scream
and now I recall lofting my shoes,
one by one, into a rapt sea attentive
to my every gesture. There they lie,
buried lives, shoestrings waving like
the arms of drunken dancers, luminous
shapes moving past like the lights
behind the eyelids of my waking friends.

Watching the Local Semi-Pro Team
with My Father

It's all in the feet, watch the catcher's feet,
he says, below the deepening blue of twilight baseball
under lights. Shattered bulbs leave a blind spot
in left field where three-fingered Ken Marler spits
Red Man as he waits, and across the pitcher's mound
a thin shadow gives the ball a flutter. On the steal
the catcher with stupid feet takes one step too many
too late. Later, when the batter pulls one out to left,
we think of how the beauty of the game improves with
distance. The white ball arcs against a blue-black sky,
and if it's gone, it's gone forever. Now Marler runs
to darkness, leaps to take it, moves it to his bad hand,
drops his glove, and with his glove-hand throws home.
Seen at this distance, it's one clean move performed
with an imagined ease. We see ourselves in the solitude
of left field: the crowd blurs, the coach waves quietly
like a departing relative. My father stands beside me,
and while the sky flattens into black, we fall to silence,
this game bearing all we have of subtlety or grace.

Describing the Back of My Hand

First the four small bumps, knuckles
they're called, and a fifth one on the thumb,
an appendage along with four fingers splayed
outward and ending in a fine hardness
that shines sometimes under lamp light,
or in movies, catching an odd glow.
Worst are the four veins running to the wrist
as if each knuckle had its own throat,
the ones you notice in times of boredom
or wonder, sitting at a concert perhaps,
your arm lying seductively alongside, fat
of the palm pressed against the cool edge
of the armrest, fingers drooping, curled
slightly, Adam reaching out to God.
And then you notice the big blue one closest in,
bulging like death beneath the pale stretched skin,
and you see the subtle, slow throbbing of the fingers.

In a Waterfront Hotel in California

On the sunporch across the way, the girl
in the brown bikini, her white-haired grandmother
with the rolled-up paperback. Neither knows
how important she is. In this scene. Against
the backdrop of their lives I keep making up.
Leontyne Price offers *Un bel di* from my stereo
this morning, *Caro nome* over cantaloupe and
scrambled eggs, but neither woman looks my way.
Their obsession is the sea, apparently, or perhaps
the blank slate of the horizon where they write
the future to include gulls, a teal blue sky,
and themselves dressed all in white, strolling
a beach where I am absent. With pages of poems
fluttering over the kitchen table, a tiny Florentine
print on the wall, nothing more, my life is obviously
for sale. I've chewed solitude like an old towel.
That whore, imagination, left before breakfast,
suggesting I meet my neighbors—dominoes, maybe,
or a game of charades. My appeal to memory
yields a stinking canal, rats floating belly up,
moonlit gondola beneath the Palazzo Falier. There
is the girl beside me quoting Browning, her grandmother
leaning from the balcony, singing coloratura death-threats.
Suddenly imagination in a brown bikini hoists herself
over the side, belching out the bad news: gray skies,
thunderstorms, anything I want except the real.

At the National Gallery: Hélène Rouart in Her Father's Study

FOR MY DAUGHTER

The light falls along the pale yellowing wall
like a thin gauze, or else my eyes are blurring,
the paintings seem to fade so. Behind this haze
Sarah Fairchild slowly forms where Hélène Rouart
stood before. Cezannes, Seurats line the walls,
but still I see your profile behind the panes
of my office door. The morning sun surrounds you
in your blue nightgown, and your newly washed
blonde hair shimmers like the far trees of these
landscapes. You are four thousand miles away,
and here in a stale wet city smelling of smoke
and the sweat of bureaucrats I cannot distract
myself with paintings I have waited twenty years
to see. Instead I see your small, frail form
hovering among my books like the bathers
of a Sunday afternoon. When I come home, one gift
will be a picture of Van Gogh's *Wheatfield and Cypress Trees.*
I will hold you in my arms, and from my study window
we will see across the field a cypress bursting into flame.

To My Friend

To my friend they all look like movie stars.
"Here comes Herbert Lom," he'll say, and a guy
in a low-angle shot looms over us, bulging
forehead shouting TREASON to pedestrians.
This history of personalities repeats itself each day.
"Take a look at ZaSu Pitts behind the pineapples"
or "Jesus, Zachary Scott sacking groceries!"
He collects them like old stills, hunts for them
in every bar, smoke-curls and clicking glasses
whispering sly promises of Sidney Greenstreet.
Or at traffic lights: Ginger Rogers in a Dodge,
Errol Flynn on a blue Suzuki. The glamour
of appearances. The way montage erases vast
ontological gaps. A wino as Quasimodo as Anthony
Quinn explains the brunette cheerleader, who is
really Gina Lollobrigida. Life connects this way,
but huge sympathies are lost in a single shot.
Sitting here in the Knox Street Tavern, I see what
he means: the inevitable crowd scene, brick street
lifted into light, flat faces rounding into possibility.
Behind the bar Eric von Stroheim smokes a Gauloise,
merciless and cool, contemplating so many frames
per second, the small darknesses we never see.

Part Three

Nothing is left
of that time beyond memories, only a faint
remembering.

CESARE PAVESE *(trans. William Arrowsmith)*

Flight

> In the early stages of epilepsy there
> occurs a characteristic dream . . . . One is
> somehow lifted free of one's own body;
> looking back one sees oneself and feels a
> sudden, maddening fear; another presence is
> entering one's own person, and there is no
> avenue of return.
>
> GEORGE STEINER

Outside my window the wasps
are making their slow circle,
dizzy flights of forage and return,
hovering among azaleas
that bob in a sluggish breeze
this humid, sun-torn morning.

Yesterday my wife held me here
as I thrashed and moaned, her hand
in my foaming mouth, and my son
saw what he was warned he might.

Last night dreams stormed my brain
in thick swirls of shame and fear.
Behind a white garage a locked shed
full of wide-eyed dolls burned,
yellow smoke boiling up in huge clumps
as I watched, feet nailed to the ground.
In dining cars white table cloths
unfolded wings and flew like gulls.
An old German in a green Homburg
sang lieder, *Mein Herz ist müde.*
In a garden in Pasadena my father
posed in Navy whites while overhead

silver dirigibles moved like great whales.
And in the narrowing tunnel
of the dream's end I flew down
onto the iron red road
of my grandfather's farm.
There was a white rail fence.
In the green meadow beyond,
a small boy walked toward me.
His smile was the moon's rim.
Across his egg-shell eyes
ran scenes from my future life,
and he embraced me like a son
or father or my lost brother.

Waiting for Sleep

Please, consider me a dream.
KAFKA

I only remember the white window
and the white shade and the white
drawcords, the light leaking through thin
muslin curtains. The rest of the room
in shadows. Shapes leaning from dark
corners and whispers from other rooms.

I listen at the window, my face
half-white in the morning light,
waiting to ascend, to be taken
by the sun's ray which will in waves
of imagined movement lift me
from this room, this white house.

But shades are drawn, doors closed,
and heavy whispers vanish into clouds
that lower over distant snow-filled forests.
Far below, branches break from trees.
We float in circles through the room
like dreams slowly leaving waking bodies.

Vuillard: The Painter Ker-Xavier Roussel and His Daughter

My blue coat must be blazing behind me.
   Vuillard painting on glue
in his slow way lightens a room already
   bright with red turning
to orange until in his eyes the drapes bloom
   and a brown cushion rises
into more orange, a grand excess of sun
   and morning flame. Leaning
into the open window, back to the sun,
   I see my white trousers
stunned with every color in the spectrum,
   dazzling rainbow of absence,
and my shadow, I know, will form a pool
   of ochre and gray. The ceiling
gives back in pale hues the blue shout of my coat,
   of the vase looming
in my periphery, and small domestic
   particulars litter
the mantel, pushed to the edge by this bourgeois
   glow. There the beginnings
of a large hearth vanish into life while
   a clock in another room
ticks dully along and shadows slide backwards
   into open windows.
When years from now I admire this painting's moment,
   this life within a life,
will I recall the flourishing this morning
   of oranges and blues
in my mind's imagining, or the darkening
   of other rooms, interiors,

where time crawls on and on? What young woman
    at my side, slender
hand on my sleeve, will recall the white bonnet
    above her face round
as a peach or small sun? Or the smile
    of her father, staring
into rooms and future rooms beyond this painted
    blue and orange one?

Cars

They were our bright lights.
At night we were stars
coming out, amazing main
street with our fluid bodies,
liquid under light, seven
coats of finish streaming by
in candy-apple red, green
flaked with gold, or
blue in six shades from
midnight to metallic.

Inside, our songs said life
was sad except for love,
which was everywhere,
like pain. *Love hard
and die young,* one sang,
so we pulled our women
closer and drove fast
to a river with a moon,
an arch of cottonwoods,
and the cicada's harsh
complaint. Flesh was easy,
but death was distant
as the spaces mirrored
in our laminated hoods.

When late that summer night
we pulled Jimmy Deeds
from his crumpled heap
on Highway 54,
we looked up at the red
light swooping through the trees

and saw how metal lay
in moonlight like sequins.
We spoke no more of love
or the other thing. And I
remember in the almost quiet
night the sudden strangeness
of our sleek and singing cars.

Ornithology

The young beg silently so as not
to attract predators to the nest . . .
this, passing before my drunken eyes
like the loose pages of memory, TV
staring through the dark room, shadows
of Ukrainian bird-life fluttering against
the wall of yellowed sheetrock like
Van Gogh's field of crows. My uncle
would have said, did in fact say,
the paralyzed truth to every lie
he ever told, truth in fact flying
out of the room like a thousand pigeons.
We dream of flight, as he did, but waking,
blinded by the sun smearing its fat lips
on the one unbroken window, find our feet
sunk in concrete, paralyzed, the truth
of our lives stuck like stones to the floor.
The young beg silently . . . their mouths
open always for the world's feast, and
then the song of the mother, sung
in terror and wisdom, and the paralyzed hope
of flight: the quick, awkward climb,
the fall, the wings loosening, giving,
the cat crouched low on the steady earth.

The Limits of My Language: English 85B

Nouns normally serve to identify
things in space, verbs to release
them in time.
JOHN FELSTEIN

The limits of my language are the
limits of my world.
LUDWIG WITTGENSTEIN

The black shawl falls from your shoulders
as you rise against your daughter's tugs
and whispers, and your withered mouth
opens in a dry quaver like voices
heard across a windblown field, *Rock of Ages,*
cleft for me, and my students wake to listen.

On that first day she whispered, warning me:
She thinks she's in church. She's my mother
and I'll have to bring her every day.
Your eyes wandered like fish behind a glass
and your crooked hand jerked back from mine.

So I've become a minister to you,
some fundamental backwoods screamer,
redeemer of Oklahoma souls, surrounded
by a choir of distant kin-folk robed
in flecks of stained-glass light and shade.
The Old Rugged Cross or *Bringing in the Sheaves*
lifts you right out of your seat at times,
and we wait while your daughter puts you
back in place: *Be quiet now, Momma.*
There's no time for that. In her voice

I hear your own among hymns hovering
on an Oklahoma Sunday years ago
inside a white frame church *let me hide
myself in thee* and in your shaken glance
and palsied hands I see you kneeling there
beneath dim memories of burnt-out fields
and black locust clouds looming down
wailing with God's own sorrow *let the water
and the blood* creek floods crawling
across gray moonlit ground, black hours
in storm cellars between dank earth walls
from thy riven side which flowed your mother
crying, the same hymns hanging in the air
like dust as you knelt there that Sunday,
clump of cinquefoil in your fist, big ribboned
Easter hat pulled back, as the preacher man
laid hands on you and promised everything:
hope, happiness, the heaven of eternal
Being.

                              And so,
through a dustbowl girlhood, a husband
headed for hell, and one daughter who turned out
right, you saved your best for last. Now
you come into my room and take your place
and stare into some space beyond these walls.
Every time I take a stick of chalk,
you see the wafer in my hand.
Every time I write a word across the board,
you see me beckon to the choir.
Every time I ask is this a verb or noun,

you turn the pages of your book.
And when I spread my arms for answers,
you rise slowly to sing, *Amazing grace,
how sweet the sound,* out of time and place.

The Houses

Houses lift and fall along hilly streets
like the lungs of the breathers inside
whose nightmares climb on black wings
as I walk by in darkness and new snow.
Only a few lights in sight, insomniacs
or neurotics wracked by bad dreams of
sad childhoods. Someone back from night
shift, waiting for the whites and pinks
of dawn to give him back the world
once more before sleep moves in with
its gaudy caravan of lost causes.
The yellow brick here, cupola and
rusted weathervane, belongs to Levin
with his woven rugs, lace, and throngs
of family photographs sprawled across
the Steinway. He dreams of history.
And Mrs. Potter, across from Sacred Heart,
claims to sleep in vast gray fields
of unbending wheat, a kind of Kansas
of the soul, where her mad daughter
always visits. Down the hill, Hermann's
Drugstore blinks its green neon, blurred
by snow gusts. In three hours everyone
is here, warmed by coffee and the year's
first snow. Dreams gather, rise, and
above the spreading dawn, five-sided
gambrel roofs, made to keep demons out,
give them back to history and weather.

Photograph

In this one you are blind-folded,
long white dress with puffed sleeves
gathering light from the window behind you.
The wood floors you waxed are pools of ice.

Arms bent hesitantly, fingers curled,
you claw air and stumble at the carpet's edge.
No one will help you. Your mother, smiling,
bends backward as your hand sweeps near. Two uncles
blow smoke clouds and show their teeth. Your father frowns.
You, in this familiar room, the stranger, the awkward guest.

What is this game? How can I, years later,
dropping this battered photograph from a book
you left behind, not see the woman in the girl,
lost, light-filled in a dark room, bodies
dumb as ghosts, the hands starting into flight?

Hitchcock

Before the lights went out, looking back
in a full house, you must have seen
old faces child-like with expectancy.
The strangest things can happen. Here.
And then you knew we wanted dreams
where all the terrors that we learned
weren't real, were real, here, in the dark:
dreams that flickered like venetian blinds
in white-frame houses where we stood
in halls with roses on the walls, stared
at doors the wind slammed shut, yelled
up stairs before we took one step,
and then another, up. And ran back down.
You took us only where we'd been
before, and then made every fear
come true. The hall that darkens
at the end, leads to darker rooms.
The door that keeps the unknown out,
lets it come in. The winding stairs
that draws us from our mothers' laps,
won't let us come back. We stand there,
looking up, and all the shrieks and
flapping wings we ever woke up from,
we wake up to. And when we leave,
glad for light outside dim movie houses,
we grow back into day and wide, white streets.

The Pleasure Drive

I need to find again, to make a life,
A child's Sunday afternoon, the Pleasure Drive
Where everything went by but time . . .
    RANDALL JARRELL

Sitting here slumped over my poached egg
and foam-rubber English muffin, I see
through screens and a gauze of morning fog
the vague blue tips of pine, poplar, every tree
planted with temporary lives in mind. I beg
to see a pin oak, each five-fingered leaf
red as Christmas candles on the Steinway,
string quartet and smell of baking bread
swelling in the air like yeast. Any Sunday
afternoon, pin oaks hysterical with red
flew past our Packard's back-seat window
where I knelt to get a view. The light chatter
of my parents I remember, and the swans
crossing the pond, its dense surface scattered
with leaves and white papers circling down
from who knows where. And then the park
thinned out to meet the river. On the river drive
I pressed my palms flat against the window.
Men in Homburgs, flashy ties, and spats would row
their young women, lithe and pale with dark
lipstick, behind the tall marsh grass. Alive
and splendid, the sun-glitter of the river,
the colored boats gliding on and on,
and my mother's silk words spilling over
the front seat, bright syllables on waves
of light and dark from tree-tunneled streets
and boulevards . . . This was, is, my one

false dream, a bright spot in my brain, life's
last lie for the very old, for a boy in West
Texas watching the Rock Island rip past:
the diner's car with white tablecloths, freight
cars flashing yellow, green, and red in late
afternoon's glare, then nothing, just land,
sky, mesquite trees black against the sand.
I used mesquite to cook with. At night, alone,
I ate rabbit, my good teeth biting to the bone.

Late Game

If this is soccer,
the moon's up for grabs.

It floats low over the goalee,
whose father waits downfield
measuring the distance,
several white lines
that flame then fade
like breaking waves.

The players pull night
behind them.
Luminous uniforms
move the white ball
quietly here, there.

Then out of these blurred
frail bodies
the ball looms.

His son's arms flash
against the moon,
catching it,

and one pale cry leaps
toward the stars.

Swimming at Menninger's

The face of an amnesiac bursts
through a splash of pink tungsten lights,
and from the edge I lift her slim,
cold body to my side. She is my friend,
and her long silences are not strange
but rather familiar fields of bending
wheat unimportant for what they hide,
easy in their plain and empty motions.
The pool is my favorite place, she says.
In memories and dreams it stays,
always, the same. And from the slow,
white silence she unwinds a story
that, like the others, I know will turn
and circle at the end: there is a map
in her head, she says, strange countries
in pastel shades, no names. There is
a country on her map where there are
only pools, each with a girl who lies
on the bottom, still and small, and never
moves. Inside each girl is another map,
another country that has only pools,
each with a girl . . .

             The road beyond
is bright with evening visitors, headlights
rounding a curve, sweeping the grounds
and lifting the dark from one moon-white
face whose eyes flash red, then vanish
in the tree line. As the last taillights
diminish in the darkness of the outer gate,
we slide back in, shuddering, and walk
in that thick way we dream so often
across the pool's blue floor. We hold

our arms out straight and teeter along
thin black stripes in the heavy water
as she repeats with every nervous step
the refrain of all her stories: *we are,*
we are, we are what we forget.

Part Four

The Arrival of the Future

> . . . the question of whether the appearing
> reality is to be understood more as the appear-
> ance of something that always is or as the
> arrival of what is future.
> WOLFHART PANNENBURG

In that country of old photographs—
men and women in overalls and work shoes,
daughters bobbing their hair like Clara Bow,
posing on the running board of a Model T—
word went out like threshing crews:
the end of the world was coming,
Judgment Day, and Christ would ride in on a cloud.

That summer
the land seemed to die beneath your hands,
iron-red clods withering apart,
dust rising
until earth was fire in your lungs.
Puffballs blew down from cottonwoods
like small shrouds.
Spiderwebs in doorways touched your lips.

They said the end was coming and you believed them.
One day the sun would die
like the flame in one of your kerosene lamps
when you walked through the house at night
mumbling your prayers,
and God's own son would descend
among seven lamps and seven stars,
His fine white raiment rippling
like the silk of a wedding dress
you remembered from eleven years ago.

Or would He, you wondered,
swoop suddenly straight down,
plucking you up in a rush of wings,
pressing you against his hard yet merciful breast?

Those weeks you stood in church,
singing the old hymns,
watching as more and more
let themselves be drowned and resurrected
before the universe collapsed,
envisioning His pale encircling arms gathering you,
your children, and all the kinfolk together
just like Thanksgiving or threshing time
or someone's funeral.

In the potato patch,
feeling a small dull pain beneath your fingernails
where the dirt packed in and hardened,
you thought again, with *Rock of Ages*
running through your head,
about the last day, and wept
for the soul of your unbaptised husband.
You looked across your Oklahoma farm
and remembered drought,
a tornado that carried my mother across the creek,
the flood when Black Bear rose,
the infant death of one child
now buried in the front yard.

And then the shadow came.
You gripped the hoe and saw the sun
begin to slide beneath some huge and moving darkness.
Chickens squawked and scuttled to the hen house.

Slowly the ground fell away
and your hand vanished in a sudden night,
and you shouted to your children in another field
not to be afraid, He was coming, it was time.

Later, when the rooster crowed
and the same day started up again,
you saw a new world almost like the old
Barn, silo, road, fence, tree-line of the creek—
everything was there but new,
with a kind of shine, you said, *brand new.*

This apocalypse you spoke of often,
smoking your clay pipe,
gazing from the front porch as night came on.
I held one fist behind another
to show the sun behind the moon,
but this was what you knew:
the strange new depth of light,
a fullness in the feel of dirt,
the air, numinous and blue,
the tide of feeling when your children were reborn
complete and waving from the other field,
your doomed husband, my grandfather,
in all his brittle strength restored.

You whispered new prayers in your rounds at night,
and when the last light had been turned off,
you touched my face in the bloom of dark.
I knew you before you knew yourself,
you said, giving me another chance to see
that this constant passage
from daylight into night,
the world removed and given back in light,
rise and fall and rise,
was forever now and new and holy.

About the Author

B.H. Fairchild was born in Houston, Texas and grew up there and in small towns in west Texas, Oklahoma, and Kansas. He attended the University of Kansas and University of Tulsa and now lives with his wife and daughter in Claremont, California. *The Arrival of the Future* was his first full-length book of poems, originally published by Swallow's Tale Press in 1985, followed by *Local Knowledge* (*Quarterly Review of Literature*) in 1991. His third book, *The Art of the Lathe*, won the Beatrice Hawley Award at Alice James Books in 1997 and was subsequently a Finalist for the 1998 National Book Award, also receiving the Kingsley Tufts Poetry Award, the William Carlos Williams Award, the PEN West Poetry Award, the California Book Award, the Natalie Ornish Poetry Award from the Texas Institute of Letters, and an Honorable Mention for the 1999 Poet's Prize. His poems have appeared in *Southern Review, Poetry, Hudson Review, Yale Review, TriQuarterly, Sewanee Review,* and other journals and in several anthologies, including *The Best American Poems of 2000.* He has been the recipient of fellowships from the National Endowment for the Arts, the Guggenheim Foundation, and the Rockefeller Foundation and is the author of *Such Holy Song,* a study of William Blake.

Notes

"Groceries": The lines quoted are from Louise Glück's poem, "The School Children," in *The House on Marshland* (New York: Ecco Press, 1975), p. 19.

"Three Poems after Photographs by Robert Frank": These photographs can be found in Frank's landmark collection, *The Americans* (New York: Grove Press, 1959).

"Flight": This poem is a dramatic monologue inspired by a passage, used as an epigraph here, from George Steiner's essay, "Humane Literacy," in *Language and Silence* (New York: Atheneum, 1977, p. 11) in which Steiner is paraphrasing Dostoevsky.

Acknowledgments

Acknowledgment is made to the following publications for poems which originally appeared in them.

The American Writer: "The Woman at the Laundromat Crying 'Mercy'"
Another Small Mazagine: "Hitchcock"
AWP Newsletter: "Swimming at Menninger's"
California Quarterly: "Cars"
Cincinnati Poetry Review: "The Robinson Hotel"
Hiram Poetry Review: "C & W Machine Works"
Kansas Quarterly: "Waiting for Sleep," "The Houses"
Memphis State Review: "Vuillard: The Painter Ker-Xavier Roussel and His Daughter"
minnesota review: "The Limits of My Language"
Montana Review: "Angels," "Watching the Local Semi-Pro Team with My Father"
National Poetry Competition Winners 1983: "To My Friend"
Negative Capability: "The Girl in the Booth"
North Dakota Quarterly: "8th Street Bar"
Outerbridge: "Black Bear Creek"
Pawn Review: "Groceries"
Poetry: "Flight"
Poetry NOW: "8th Street"
Puerto del Sol: "The Men"
Southern Poetry Review: "The Arrival of the Future," "Night Shift," "Portrait of My Father as a Young Man"
Sulphur River: "The PLAZA"
Swallow's Tale Magazine: "At the National Gallery: Hélène Rouart in Her Father's Study," "Hair," "The Pleasure Drive"
Texas Review: "Describing the Back of My Hand," "Late Game"
"Machine Shop with Wheat Field" and "In the Homes of the Working Class" first appeared, and others were reprinted, in *C & W Machine Works* (a limited edition chapbook, Denton, Texas: Trilobite Press, 1983), and several other poems were reprinted in *Flight* (a limited edition chapbook, Elgin, South Carolina: Devil's Millhopper Press, 1985).
"Late Game," "8th Street Bar," "The Robinson Hotel," and "Hair" were reprinted in *The Anthology of Magazine Verse & Yearbook of American Poetry* (Monitor Book Co., 1981, 1984, 1985).
"Swimming at Menninger's" was an Associated Writing Programs Anniversary Awards Winner in 1983, "The Woman at the Laundromat Crying 'Mercy'" received first prize in the 1984 Santa Cruz Writers' Union poetry competition, and "Waiting for Sleep" received the 1984 Seaton Poetry Award from *Kansas Quarterly*.

Recent Titles from Alice James Books

ALICE JAMES BOOKS has been publishing books since 1973. One of the few presses in the country that is run collectively, the cooperative selects manuscripts for publication through competitions. New authors become active members of the press, participating in editorial and production activities. The press, which places an emphasis on publishing women poets, was named for Alice James, sister of William and Henry, whose gift for writing was ignored and whose fine journal did not appear until after her death.

Typeset and designed by Lisa Clark
Printing by Thomson-Shore